Fiddler's Hill
and other stories

John Broughton

Fiddler's Hill	2
Jack Frost and the Sandman	12
The Bells of Acorn Tumbling	23
Once Upon a Barren Moor	38
Roderick's Remarkable Home-made Honey	53

Nelson

Fiddler's Hill

Most rabbits were to be found at Fiddler's Hill, where no man dared to tread. Little Walter came as daylight faded and twilight was turning the trees to eerie shapes. Fiddler's Hill grew menacing with the night, and dusk made the brooding circle of standing stones at its foot seem to be figures eager to escape. Walter shivered and started at every sound, because his father did not allow him to come here. His traps set, the boy was ready to return home.

At this moment the quaintest figure slipped ghost-like beyond the trees. It was the shade of a man in old-fashioned clothes. He wore a faded tunic and his piercing quicksilver eyes matched the moonbeams darting in the glade. His fiddle played an enchanting tune, casting colours into the evening gloom. Behind him a procession of imps frisked and pranced, their mischievous faces alight with glee at the phantom fiddler's artistry.

The boy could not fight the beautiful sound of the fiddler's spell, which lured him in a trance towards the hill. One of his rabbit traps snapped cruelly across his worn shoe and, mercifully, pain drove the magic music from his ears. Struggling free, Walter glanced fearfully towards the glade; but the cheerless hill and the brooding stones stood in empty silence.

Walter wondered whether he had been dreaming or whether it had been a trick of the light. He stood in thought, until a sad owl hooting solemnly from the rustling leaves reminded him that it was past time for home. Still trembling, Walter limped away from Fiddler's Hill.

In the morning Walter's reward was two fat rabbits from the hill and so he decided to return with his traps that same evening. This time though, just to be sure, Walter filled his ears with sealing wax. The wax could not stop his heart thumping wildly against his breast, as from the forest's edge he once again saw the weirdest sight. In flitting light, the fiddler skipped through the glade with frenzied imps dancing at his feet. In terror Walter watched them until suddenly they vanished deep inside Fiddler's Hill.

The hill proved to be a fine place for rabbits as the days passed by and Walter's family had plenty to eat. Whenever his father asked how Walter did so well, the boy would say nothing and simply smile. Every evening the wax kept Walter safe and from among the trees he'd watch and copy the fiddler's flickering hand, unknowingly learning the phantom's magic art.

One afternoon a tinker called at Walter's house. He had tramped deep into the forest on his travels. Saucepans swung from his pack and his floppy hat hung down over his curly beard. He showed Walter's mother all his wares, spreading a dazzling collection of ribbons, buttons and silks before her. They both listened

eagerly to his tales from the city, where forest people seldom visited, and Walter decided that one day he would go to the city too. The tinker chatted on and Walter slipped away unnoticed with his traps to Fiddler's Hill.

In the half-light, all mist and moonlight, the fiddler played his lilting tunes. As usual Walter copied the fiddler's every move; he was no longer frightened, as he had become so used to the strange scene.

But his heart nearly stopped as a heavy boot trod on his hand; with wax in his ears he had not heard the wandering tinker's crashing steps. Spellbound by the sweet music the tinker strode past with his bulky pack, eyes glazed and staring. Walter watched dumbly as the poor tinker reached Fiddler's Hill. A beam of moonlight bathed the tinker, instantly turning him to stone. A cold smile crossed the fiddler's faint white face and his flickering hand dropped still by his side. Cackling with delight the imps joined hands, prancing and skipping around the stone which now concealed the tinker's shape. In a panic Walter ran for home: nothing would persuade him to return to Fiddler's Hill.

Instead he wandered round near his home, pretending that two sticks were a fiddle and

bow. For hours his fingers played restlessly across the sticks, until his father noticed and brought his son indoors, where he pulled an old fiddle and horsehair bow from a chest. Little Walter played the haunting melodies he'd learned by moonlight in the glade. The woodman and his wife were enchanted by the beauty of the sound and could not move a muscle while he played. Coloured stars lit their minds and filled them with great happiness. When Walter laid down the bow they questioned him closely as to how he'd learned such wonderful skill: but little Walter just smiled and turned away.

Since his father fell into a trance whenever Walter played, the boy had to wander off among the trees so that some work could be done. Woodland birds hushed their songs and calls at his wonderful playing and gathered to fill the sun-soaked tree tops above him. But not only birds were drawn by the magic tunes; Walter stared and an imp stared back! Walter blinked, but the imp could not because it had turned to stone and toppled slowly from a branch to the carpet of leaves below.

Very worried, Walter dashed indoors and carried on playing there, where he felt safe. But before long his father came in, axe in one hand and stone imp in the other.

"I found this ornament by the door. Is it yours, Walter?" the woodman asked.

"No!" cried Walter, and ran upstairs.

Lying on his bed, Walter thought hard until the answers came. Knowing now what he must do, Walter set off for Fiddler's Hill. He had never been there in daylight before. Now he strode bravely with his old fiddle to the top of the hill. There was no movement in the sun-drenched glade, only the stillness of the standing stones. Walter slowly raised his fiddle and played one of the secret moonlight tunes.

At once an uproar shattered the silence of the forest glade: from the heart of Fiddler's Hill a frightful shrieking and wailing was unloosed. At the foot of the hill the tinker stood blinking in the midday sun. He watched the other stones turn slowly back into the people they really were. From deep within the hill, the weird sound of snapping fiddle strings finally left all silent underground.

Walter stopped playing, but the oddest collection of people mobbed him with their excited questions. Walter simply entranced them with a magic tune and skipped off, leading them out through the trees. Behind him the spellbound procession danced and swayed, while overhead the sky was full of the fluttering wings of birds captive to the beautiful melody.

Explanation dragged on in the woodman's little home for hours. Merchants speaking in old-fashioned tongues (for they had been petrified for hundreds of years) eagerly pressed gold into Walter's small hand as thanks for freeing them from the fiddler's ancient spell.

When he was old enough, years later, Walter set off to explore from city to city. In the cities, the cathedral squares thronged with people eager to hear his enchanting tunes. As they listened, their hearts swelled with great happiness and they showered coins at Walter's feet. Cheering crowds often asked him to play on into the night, but wisely Walter always shook his head; for not only were *people* drawn to his beautiful tunes, as you may easily see on any cathedral wall.

Jack Frost and the Sandman

Sharp eyes spied the turquoise horn of a white unicorn as it frolicked beneath the ice mountains. From nowhere Jack Frost leaped upon the unicorn's back and tamed him with his cruel fingernails. On a unicorn, Jack's mischief would know no bounds. He smiled frostily at the fading day and his fingers itched to nip the tender primroses of spring.

They left the icelands far behind, galloping to the distant world where humans live, and coming at last to an old town of narrow streets and crooked houses. There, in the oldest house with uneven floors, a young boy shivered between his sheets. Adam hoped he'd only imagined the sharp face at his window, which had given him restless wintry dreams.

Galloping backwards and forwards at amazing speed, Jack spread an icy cloak wherever he passed, and from each house he dangled twisted icicles shaped just like his unicorn's horn. At daybreak, from the dark edge of a nearby pine forest, he giggled at the poor townspeople as they repaired burst water pipes and rescued pitiful ducks from the frozen pond. Adam brushed ice from his donkey's fur and covered the poor numb beast with a patchwork blanket.

Jack Frost wasted no time the following night. He loved to make everywhere bitterly cold and frosty white, so he soon had the moonlit town shimmering with ice crystals. The wood-planked doors splintered silently before the unicorn's horn and inside log fires died at Jack's freezing touch. With the tip of his horn the unicorn painted beautiful pictures of icy mountains on the windows, as he was terribly homesick and fretful under his cruel new master.

Meanwhile Jack hurriedly piled frost onto beds and grinned as little children grew chilled. As they lay asleep he pinched their toes with icy fingers and left them wailing as he galloped unseen away. Behind him the whole wakeful town battled with the unexpected cold.

The townspeople mended their doors and

strengthened them with extra wood. They had no idea what could possibly have caused the trouble. They doubled their blankets and heaped logs onto their fires. But silently at midnight Jack struck again, draping icicles from sagging lampshades.

Meanwhile across the crackling ground a lonely figure walked into town. The stranger marvelled at the magic cast upon the glittering white streets; he had never seen frost like this before, though he always travelled at night. Moreover it wasn't even winter. How could such weather come in spring? The stranger was a good judge, because his work took him to many lands, performing his sandman duties. The Sandman wore a curious yellow coat and carried a heavy sack upon his shoulder.

The Sandman peeped inside the crooked houses and was amazed that he could see his breath indoors. The tired, black-ringed eyes of the tiny children brought a frown to his kindly face. The Sandman gazed sadly at children huddled restlessly, in fitful sleep, under their frosty blankets. He slipped quietly from house to house casting a grain of sand from his sack into each child's eyes. Magically, their eyelids grew heavy and their sleep deepened, for this

was the Sandman's special work. He soon had all the fires blazing away, making the little houses warm and cosy once more.

When he had finished, the Sandman sat in a chimney nook to puzzle over the problem. As a rule he visited these children once a week to check their sleep; yet he had never known it so cold before, especially in spring. The Sandman's eyes strayed to the window: in beautiful frosty pictures he read the unicorn's sorrowful tale. It told of the icelands far away and of its own capture by Jack Frost. In fairy lines of frozen ice the unicorn had sketched all of Jack's wicked deeds for anyone who cared to see them. The Sandman leaped to his feet and seized a gnarled walking stick from by the door. In the stable he mounted a trembling donkey wrapped in a patchwork blanket: the Sandman was determined to find and beat Jack Frost.

All this time, Jack had been amusing himself at an outlying farm. He was nipping piglets and giggling at their frightened squeals. At last, Jack grew bored with this game and looked up to see the smoke curling from the shadowed little houses. He was not at all pleased as he, of course, preferred to think of chilblained people shivering inside their freezing homes.

Jack galloped madly back to town to discover what had gone wrong. From the opposite direction the Sandman's donkey crackled across the frozen rutted road. Jack Frost's keen eye spotted the Sandman's yellow coat and he recognized an old enemy. He charged the

unicorn cruelly forward and the donkey took one look at the unicorn's glinting icy horn and turned to race back to town. The Sandman clung on grimly as he was no horseman and no donkey had ever moved so fast before.

Jack Frost galloped cackling behind until, just before the donkey's stable, the icy horn struck the Sandman to the ground. Luckily the deadly ice horn only pierced his sack, spilling magic sand upon the frozen ground. As he fell, the Sandman gave the unicorn a mighty whack with the gnarled walking stick. The unicorn bolted and even Jack's fierce fingernails could not stop him until they reached the forest's edge.

Dazed, the Sandman stumbled off, moments before the door of the oldest house creaked open. The commotion had brought Adam out before dawn. The youngster pulled his dressing gown tighter and glanced about the moon-drenched yard. He could not understand why his donkey was panting in the stable and the stable door stood open, when everything was still. Then his eye chanced upon the split sack of sand. He wandered over to have a look and, seeing nothing special about it and being a thoughtful lad, he began to scatter it upon the icy footpath so that his shaky old grandmother would not slip in the morning.

Adam was working away, when suddenly he felt cold eyes upon him. He looked up to see an icy figure upon a unicorn almost near enough to touch. They stood motionless, staring at one another across the frozen cobbles. Jack Frost laughed wickedly and charged the unicorn straight at the little boy's chest. Bravely Adam stood his ground and flung his only weapon straight into Jack Frost's eyes. The magic sand did its job: before Jack hit the ground he was fast asleep. At last the unicorn was free and in a flash he left Jack's cruel fingernails behind forever, as he sped off through the night to his homeland of the icy peaks.

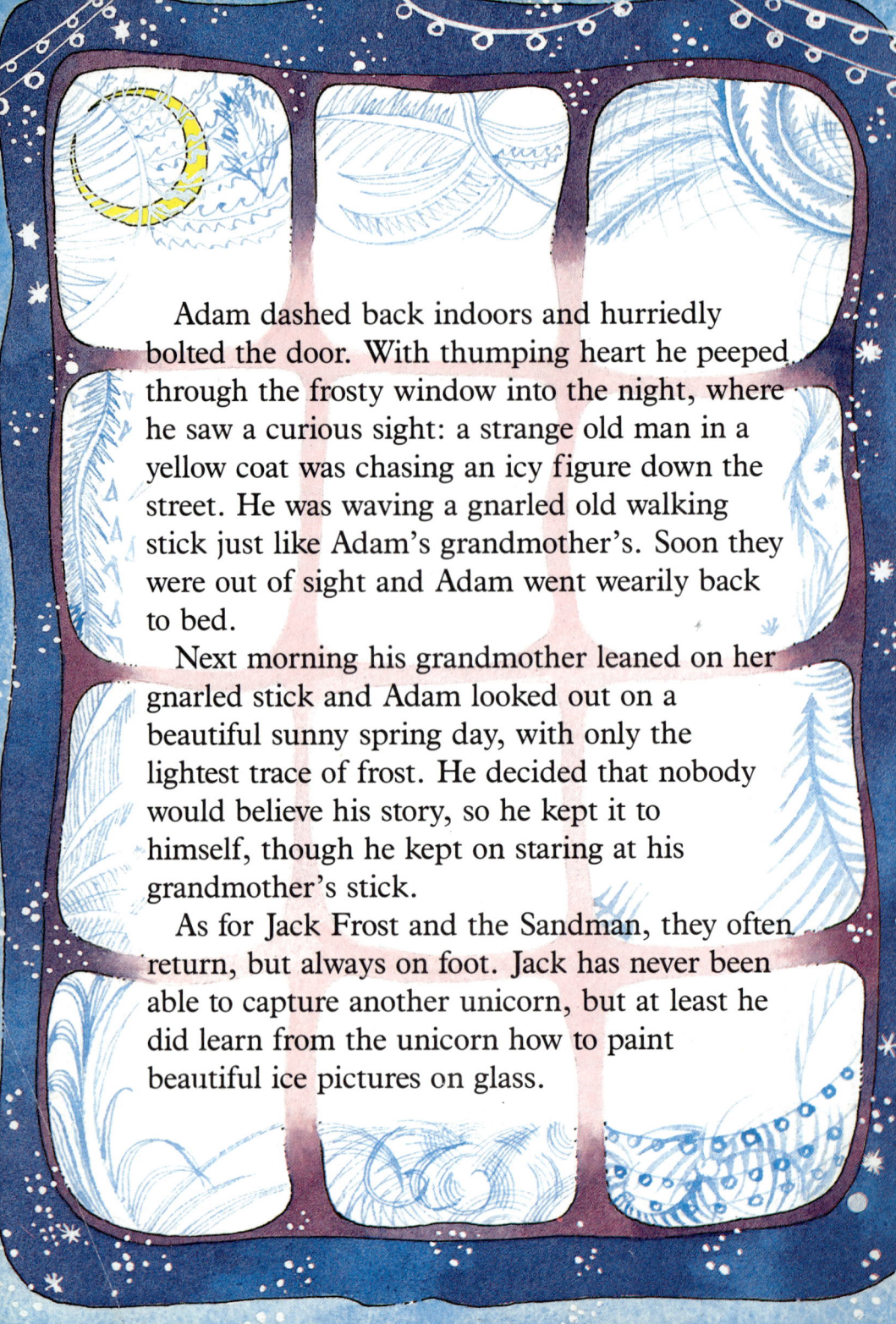

Adam dashed back indoors and hurriedly bolted the door. With thumping heart he peeped through the frosty window into the night, where he saw a curious sight: a strange old man in a yellow coat was chasing an icy figure down the street. He was waving a gnarled old walking stick just like Adam's grandmother's. Soon they were out of sight and Adam went wearily back to bed.

Next morning his grandmother leaned on her gnarled stick and Adam looked out on a beautiful sunny spring day, with only the lightest trace of frost. He decided that nobody would believe his story, so he kept it to himself, though he kept on staring at his grandmother's stick.

As for Jack Frost and the Sandman, they often return, but always on foot. Jack has never been able to capture another unicorn, but at least he did learn from the unicorn how to paint beautiful ice pictures on glass.

The Bells of Acorn Tumbling

Oscar Digweed made his fortune from boot polish. After money, Digweed liked polish best: beeswax, French polish, stove blacking, silver polish; just as long as it made things gleam, Oscar Digweed loved it.

Strange then, how Digweed himself should be such a dull man. He wore gloomy grey clothes and absolutely never smiled. In fact, his shoes were the only sparkling things about him. People asked one another why such a rich man should be so terribly grim. It was true that he had no wife, but he had his son Stanley to cheer him up, and his fine house next to the gasworks, by the black canal.

It came as a great surprise to Stanley when his father sold up and moved to the fresh country air, to the sleepy little village of Acorn Tumbling.

They had not been there so long, because Oscar Digweed was still clearing the cupboards, when from right at the back of the deepest cupboard in his new home, Digweed found an old box. Its lid was dusty and flaking, but inside was a beautiful set of handbells. He carried them downstairs, where he cleaned them lovingly with silver polish for hours and hours, until he could see his own gloomy face quite clearly in the glittering bells.

Oscar Digweed was not musical (music was a little too cheerful for his taste) so he did not try to play the bells. Instead, he took off his grey overalls, pulled on his black coat, and went off to see the vicar.

"I've read about them, of course," the vicar said, twirling his pointed moustache. "They have been missing for over two hundred years."

Oscar Digweed returned the bells to their rightful owner and thought no more of the matter. But soon Digweed received an invitation which was to change his entire life:

To: Mr Oscar Digweed and son.
Please come to
A Concert of Handbell Ringing
to be given by the
Choirboys of St. Elmo's Church
Acorn Tumbling.

Oscar Digweed frowned till his eyes crossed. He sighed, shrugged his shoulders, and thought it was his duty to go, even though he hated concerts or any such occasion. Stanley, on the other hand, jumped up and down clapping his hands, saying that it would be wonderful.

On the night, Stanley followed his father's miserable footsteps to the place of honour at the front of the hall. In a long boring speech the vicar told the whole village about the bells and of Mr Digweed's generosity; Digweed scowled and slumped in his chair, sighing loudly when the choirboys began to play the silver bells, which had remained hidden for so long.

Ding Dong Dingetty — Clonk!

The leather thongs holding the clappers had rotted with age. A clapper flew straight past Oscar Digweed's ear and, though the choirboys carried on bravely, three more clappers winged dangerously through the air. Choirboys were trying to ring empty bells and the vicar looked shocked. The whole village was there and it was stunned; but the biggest shock was for Stanley, who was ten years old. For ten whole years he had never seen his father smile, but here he was, grim old Oscar Digweed, on the front row, rolling with laughter in his seat. At that very moment, with tears streaming down his cheeks, Oscar Digweed first discovered his unknown love for bells.

As the days passed by, Stanley noticed a change come over his father. Occasionally he would catch him smiling! Stanley was a bright boy and it didn't take him long to work out that Digweed smiled whenever a bell chimed. His father had taken to wearing a blue suit too; Stanley thought it made a nice change after ten years of grey ones.

From time to time, Oscar Digweed would return from a trip to the city looking very pleased with himself. Regular as clockwork

(as you might expect if you could see through crates), large interesting wooden crates would arrive at the railway station. Each was marked 'FRAGILE. O. Digweed Esq., The Mansion, Acorn Tumbling.'

The villagers were quite beside themselves with curiosity, wondering what could be inside the wooden crates. It took Mrs Jackson, the village gossip, to find an excuse for calling at the Mansion before the truth came out.

"It's deafening in Digweed's house," she whispered. "There are clocks everywhere. Eighteen on the sideboard, I counted them myself, and he's got hundreds more around the house. You'd never believe the din, dear, when they chimed the hour. I can't imagine how that poor little boy manages, truly I can't."

Oscar Digweed was clearly delighted with his new hobby.

Workmen were seen to place an extra-large chiming clock on his roof, which could be seen from any part of the garden, or rather, as Digweed preferred, *heard* from any part of the garden. He fixed a highly polished bell around his horse's neck and little tinkling bells to his three white cats. He even offered to fit Stanley a bell around his neck and Stanley wasn't too sure whether his father was joking or not. Oscar Digweed even built a chiming clock onto his bird-house, which scared the birds away every fifteen minutes.

Before long, work started on a new clock tower in the market square, all paid for, of course, by Oscar Digweed. It was very grand, standing over ten metres high, with a huge clock face. It chimed each quarter hour, and on the hour a door opened allowing a big bell to swing slowly out. There also swung out a metal statue with a huge hammer to strike the time. Everyone in Acorn Tumbling agreed it was very beautiful and they all stopped whatever they were doing on market day, specially to watch the clock chime the hour.

For the first time in his life Stanley was fond of his father, because he had lost his old grimness and was always smiling. But Acorn Tumbling had changed too, for where once steam trains had hooted at level crossings, now they bonged. A gentle stroll along the peaceful lanes was not peaceful any more. There were cowbells in the meadows, not to mention the new-fangled sheepbells.

People were beginning to grumble among themselves:

"Things have changed since Digweed came."

"Digweed? The name rings a bell."

"There's a ringing in my ears all the time."

"Digweed's got builders at his place again. Wonder what he's up to now?"

Yet even the grumblers were thunderstruck at the sight soon to appear in the High Street. A slow-moving wagon creaked and groaned under a massive weight. Crowds began to gather, but

they could not quite make out the enormous object which glittered brightly in the low evening sun. They could all see how the driver had to shout and whip his horses to greater effort. The wagon jostled and pitched along the uneven road and, as it drew nearer, little boys ran to meet it before dashing back in an excited gang to the High Street.

"It's a bell, it's a bell!" they yelled. "An enormous, huge, monster bell!"

"Yes," said Stanley, who had come out to play, "that's my father's."

True enough, the wagon ground past, carrying the largest brass bell that any of them had ever seen. It turned slowly in through Digweed's brightly polished ornamental gates. For a while carpenters came and went, until the village had almost forgotten about the bell. Chuckling to himself, wearing his bright red suit with yellow waistcoat, Oscar Digweed looked lovingly up at his shining bell, swinging gently from its new wooden tower. Just in time, Stanley dived onto his bed and thrust his head under his pillow. After a busy life as boot polish manufacturer, Oscar Digweed had finally found true happiness: he could chime out the time to his heart's content.

The sound of the bell boomed around the town, rattling windows and frightening babies. Digweed's bell was not just heard in the next village: it was heard in the next valley. The village chemist soon sold out of cotton wool and wax earplugs, and people couldn't stop for a chat any more, because they all had something in their ears. Now they had to be satisfied with a nod and a wave. Acorn Tumbling was now the noisiest village in England. Even cheerful little Stanley wandered round with a miserable headache. In fact, the only happy person in Acorn Tumbling was the man who was causing all the noise.

The mayor had to call an emergency meeting. People knew it was an emergency when they saw him wearing his official hat and chain. The mayor had been talking for five minutes before he realised that nobody could hear him. He put up a sign which read:

TAKE OUT YOUR EARPLUGS.

"As I was saying," the mayor continued, "Digweed's gone too far. Enough is enough, that bell will have to go!"

The mayor paused for breath, which was as well, because Digweed chimed two o'clock on his giant bell. Plaster fell from the Town Hall ceilings as the building shook, showering the meeting in fine dust. The villagers coughed and spluttered and angry fists were raised towards Digweed's house: tempers were becoming frayed. The mayor spoke again (it was safe to speak at three minutes past two), but his words were drowned by those around him.

"Digweed out!" shouted an angry farmer waving his gun.

"But he's a nice man!" shouted the vicar.

"Bells, bells, bells! That's all he ever thinks about."

"Oh, I dong know!"

Finally it was decided that a small group of villagers, to be led by the mayor himself, should go at once to speak sternly with Mr Digweed.

As they approached Digweed's huge polished gates, the market clock chimed, and the mayor stuck his fingers in his ears just in time, for Oscar Digweed was about to chime the hour on his giant bell. They noticed some movement from beneath an upturned wheelbarrow — it looked like Stanley with his hands over his ears.

Digweed pulled once — DONG — the ground trembled; he pulled twice — DONG — and the whole village shook.

He pulled a third time and the giant bell came away, spinning through the air in a perfect arc. It buried itself into the ground exactly and entirely over Digweed, trapping its startled owner inside.

Stanley's eyes peered round as saucers from beneath the barrow.

"Help! Get me out!" came a muffled voice from within the bell.

"Just a minute," muttered the mayor craftily, "let's not be too hasty here."

Oscar Digweed was told that he'd have to stay where he was, unless he'd agree to get rid of the bells. A broken voice was heard to agree from under the bell. All the strongest men of Acorn Tumbling were called — the entire Acorn Tumbling tug-of-war team, in fact. They fastened a rope to the top of the bell and tugged for all they were worth, but they could not budge the giant bell. The farmer came leading two prize bulls by the nose. But even the entire tug-of-war team and the prize bulls could not shift the giant bell.

"Do hurry up, it's stuffy in here and dark," a little voice pleaded from within the bell.

"I've heard of a person having a voice like a bell, but never of a bell having a voice like a person!" the mayor laughed, pretending he wasn't worried.

It was then that Stanley had his bright idea.

"Bring some spades and shovels," he called, "and some wooden props."

It took until the market clock struck eight before Oscar Digweed, dirty and sticky, crawled like a giant red mole out of the tunnel under the edge of the bell. He growled to his rescuers, "I've had quite enough of bells. Come along, Stanley," and with that he hung his head and walked miserably indoors.

Oscar Digweed was rarely seen out and about after that. On the odd occasion when he did appear he would merely grunt and scowl when spoken to. It was as if his own black shadow had risen up and was walking about in his place. Oscar Digweed had never been so grim in all his very grim life, not even when he lived by the black canal. All the villagers felt sorry for Oscar Digweed for, despite the bells, they had liked him when he was cheerful.

At last, Stanley thought of the answer. One night a group of the village folk crept into Digweed's garden. They worked silently through the night with spades and hoes, planting bulbs and weeding everything except creeping campanula and nettle-leaved bellflowers. When they had finished, they left as quietly as they had come.

At last, when spring arrived in Acorn Tumbling, poor gloomy Oscar Digweed had a wonderful surprise. To his delight, his garden was ablaze with beautiful colours. Deep blue harebells spread in a carpet below his apple trees, while white snowdrops danced round joyous tulips. Beneath his windows, stately foxgloves gently nodded in the breeze. With his arm round Stanley's shoulder, Oscar Digweed stood happily in a sea of coloured bells. And not one of them spoiled the peace and quiet of Acorn Tumbling.

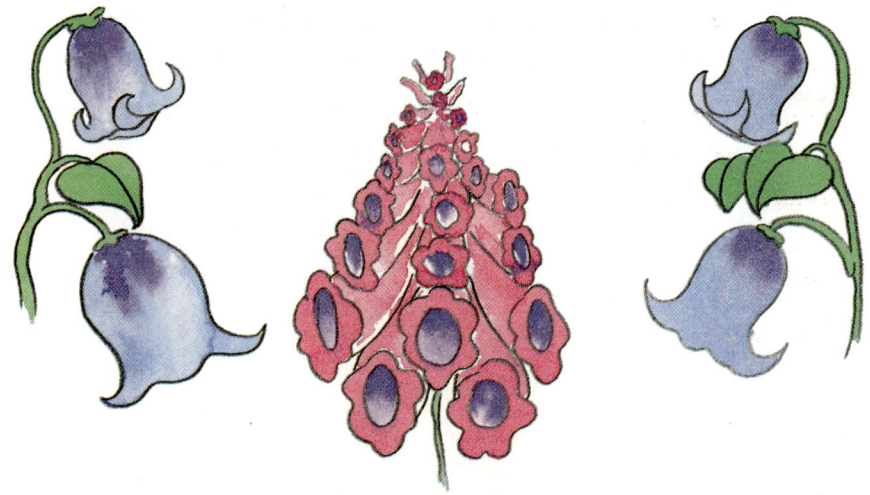

Once Upon a Barren Moor

Once upon a barren moor
There lived a bear who met a boar;
The bear he could not bear the boar
Who proved to be a dreary bore.
At last the bear could bear no more
That boar that bored him on the moor,
And so from that poor barren spot
He sent the boar on a Baron plot!

Once upon a barren moor, through rough and tumble heather, tramped a fiddler and his dancing bear. Together they travelled far and wide, across the wildest of places, looking for towns where they could play. Simon the Fiddler's wonderful tunes soon drew clapping, cheering crowds, while the bear danced among the people, collecting small coins in his master's cap.

From the edge of the moor they looked down upon the little town of High Dudgeon. Simon had never been to High Dudgeon before, so he was not to know that the people there had no coins, not even small ones: Baron de Bludge saw to that.

Down in the market square, Simon began to play and timidly, one by one, the people came out to listen until they were a huge cheering crowd. The people of High Dudgeon had not had a good time for ages — they had almost forgotten how to laugh: Baron de Bludge saw to that as well. Yet here they were, dancing and singing, having fun with Simon the Fiddler and his dancing bear.

In an instant the crowd had gone, vanished like snow on water. Simon blinked and his bear stood still. There wasn't even one coin in his master's cap. One minute there had been a swaying, jostling crowd, the next the square was completely silent. Well, not quite silent, for the air was heavy with the sound of horses' hooves. In a moment Simon was surrounded by knights on black horses. On their shields were three boars' heads and on their faces were wicked grins. Simon did not try to run, as he had not heard of Baron de Bludge . . . yet. They roped Simon and his bear behind their black horses, dragging them up to the Baron's castle.

Baron de Bludge was leaning against a whipping-post, his thick black moustache hiding an unpleasant smile. Simon noticed at once that the Baron was not polite with guests, but luckily

they had caught him in a good mood.

"Sling that wretch into the dungeon," the Baron sneered, "and chain the bear to the wall."

As it happened, the Baron's two favourite sports were boar-hunting (which he was bored with) and bear-baiting. By chance, he was right out of bears (the forest was bare of bears), until now. The Baron could not wait to start. He had the bear whipped along to his bear-garden and chained to a post by the leg.

"Gather round, everyone," the Baron called. "Fetch a hogshead of mead and a platter of eels — oh, and my foul-tempered wolfhounds; now we'll have a merry sport!"

The bear tried to dance a little jig to please the crowd, but it was no use without music and with a heavy chain on his leg. He was puzzled when the crowd began to cheer four vicious-looking shaggy hounds which weren't even dancing. He looked round for Simon, but could not see his master anywhere.

"Release the hounds!" the Baron cried, and the bear was set upon by snarling hounds.

The more they snapped and dodged his angry swipes, the more the Baron and his crowd loved it. Now as a rule, he was a peaceful bear, but this was not his idea of a pleasant picnic.

His rage grew as he struggled mightily against the chain to reach the tormenting hounds. The Baron, who had been rocking in his seat with laughter, nearly choked on an eel. His face turned from bright red to purple as ladies screamed and servants tripped over fleeing hounds. In his fury, the bear had snapped the chain. Free now, he tipped the Baron into a holly bush, before lumbering off through the castle gate. By the time everyone had calmed down, the bear was safely out of town.

He lived a lonely life on the barren moor, in a den under jagged rocks. Time and again, usually after a heavy breakfast of slow-worms, the bear would think of his poor master. At times like this, he would twirl and spin and feel extra lonely.

How great was his surprise therefore, on coming back to his den one day, to find two eyes shining from within.

"Out!" roared the bear.

"Oink!" from the den.

The bear reached in and hauled out a boar whose razor-sharp tusks curled wickedly over his lips. But the boar was too miserable to fight and, hanging his bristly head, would have slunk away.

"Wait, shouldn't you be in the forest?" asked the bear, who was a curious bear.

Before long, the boar was back in the den, sharing a supper of white ants, which the bear had been saving for a special occasion.

"Not a patch on forest worms," grumbled the boorish boar.

"Now tell me about your adventures," roared the bear, ignoring the boar's bad manners. "And don't miss anything out. I *do* love a good story."

The boar droned on for hours. The bear tried to stay awake out of politeness. He had rarely yawned so much; it really was a boring story.

"So," said the bear, "let me see, you were driven out of the forest for being so boring. Well, we'll see what we can do tomorrow."

The bear thought that he'd be going to sleep then, but the boar grumbled that the den was not lined with moss; he grumbled that he was hungry, that he was cold, and that there was not room for two. In fact, he grumbled on and on through the night, until the bear stuck bilberry roots in his ears in order to get any sleep at all.

Over a good breakfast of slow-worms, the bear gave the boar a talking-to.

"Listen, Boar, it's no wonder the other boars drove you away. There's no excuse for being *that* boring. All you need to do is amuse the other boars with exciting tales from your life."

"But nothing exciting ever happens to me," sniffed the boar gloomily, "except *I've been hunted by riders!* They chased me through the forest, carrying spears and shields. I remember, one of them yelled 'What a fat juicy one, we'll stuff an apple in his mouth and roast him!'... I was terrified, I'll tell you. Good job I can run. The one with a black moustache blew a horn. He had a shield with three boars' heads on it..."

"Boars' heads, did you say?" the bear roared, looking extremely angry. "Yes, three boars' heads," said the startled boar. "Quite bad taste if you ask me."

"Baron de Bludge!" the bear roared fiercely. "That's Baron de Bludge's shield you're talking about. He's the one who ended my dancing days." He told the boar all about the bear-garden and ended by adding sadly that he hadn't as much as sniffed honey from that day to this.

"Listen, Boar," growled the bear, and his eyes shone brightly, "I have a plan to teach the Baron a lesson and to stop you being boring all at the same time."

That night, under cover of darkness, they left the barren moor for the depths of the forest. By day, from the edge of the forest, they watched the Baron's castle for many an hour. The boar and the bear saw how cruel the Baron was to his people, who were poor and not even allowed wood for their fires. They learned which days the Baron went hunting and on which days he stayed at home.

The bear searched the forest until he found a bear-pit, specially dug by the Baron's men, craftily covered with twigs and grass for unsuspecting bears to fall into.

One Wednesday when, as usual, Baron de Bludge rode alone with his hawk by the forest's edge (the Baron loved to set his fierce hawk after timid little sparrows), out of the forest trotted the boar, almost up to the Baron's horse.

"Oink!" he grunted in his loudest voice.

"A boar!" bellowed the cruel Baron, startling the hawk right off his arm. The boar turned and ran as fast as he could into the forest. The Baron galloped headlong after him, waving his sword. He couldn't resist an unexpected boar hunt. The boar sped past the very edge of the hidden pit, but the Baron galloped straight towards it. At the very last second, the Baron's horse stopped suddenly, but the Baron carried on: over the horse's mane he sailed, smashing with a helpless wail into the deep bear-pit. There he lay in a dazed heap at the bottom.

When Baron de Bludge looked up, the strangest sight met his eyes. Above him, in a circle looking down, were thirty boars. Behind them, leaping and dancing and waving the Baron's own sword, was a familiar-looking bear.

"Help!" cried Baron de Bludge, who had never been frightened before. The bear flung the sword high over the tree tops and then, to the Baron's surprise, reached down into the pit and hauled him out.

The boars looked very angry, so the Baron made a dash for it. Even though he wasn't wearing armour, he was far slower than the huge pack of boars. They slashed at the Baron's cloak, they slashed at his clothes with razor-sharp tusks; yet, it seemed they were careful not to hurt the Baron himself. Still, he was terrified and, with clothes no more than tattered rags, he plunged gratefully into a stream. The boars followed on the bank, as Baron de Bludge waded exhausted along the stream. Once or twice, he disappeared into the icy cold water as he stumbled upon a hole in the riverbed. It seemed he had no choice but to slither out onto the opposite muddy bank. Off he staggered, lost, into the dark forest.

Night had closed in before the Baron left the

forest for the welcome lights of High Dudgeon Castle. He called from under the grey stone walls, "I'm Baron de Bludge! Let me in!"

The guards took one look at the sorry beggar below and chuckled, "If you're the Baron, I'm the King!"

No matter how he raged or threatened them, the guards stuck to the Baron's own rule: 'No strangers allowed in after dark!'

At last, the Baron gave up. Cold and hungry, dirty and tired, the Baron sat on the damp grass under the walls. At the edge of the forest thirty pairs of eyes glowed brightly from the trees. Under the stars, the Baron shivered and began to think. He did not like being poor and cold and he did not like being hunted. By morning, the Baron was a changed man. His people found him fast asleep against the wall. They wanted to know what had become of him and the Baron told them the truth, which was something he wasn't used to doing.

Baron de Bludge never hunted boars, baited bears, or even went hawking again. Strangers were allowed into the castle, day or night, and the Baron's people had plenty of food and wood in High Dudgeon. In fact, the Baron became known there as Good Baron de Bludge.

The boar became a hero with the other boars and no matter how long or how dully he told the tale of the Baron's downfall, the others never found it boring and always asked for more.

As for Simon the Fiddler, the Baron held a feast in his honour, where Simon played to cheering crowds and his bear held Simon's cap for the Baron to fill with gold. Best of all, the next time the Baron rode out in High Dudgeon, people noticed the design on his shield had changed. Gone were the three boars' heads and in their place was a jolly dancing bear.

Roderick's Remarkable Home-made Honey

Not so long ago, two friendly farmers lived close together by the banks of the River Slyme. Roderick and Osbert were depressingly poor, as their neighbouring land was nothing more than rough pasture of buttercups and clover. Roderick dreamed of one day becoming a barley farmer and Osbert spent the long summers imagining a golden landscape of wheat fields instead of his patchy green meadows. The truth was, neither could grow crops on the swampy land and without crops, they could not afford cows. Indeed, the only livestock they had was a couple of goats, a few hens and, of course, their bees. Osbert and Roderick both sold honey to anyone who chanced to stop by.

Unfortunately, although the River Slyme was always busy with travellers and traders plying to and fro, none of them ever gave the two poor farmers a second thought. Occasionally a traveller, sunbathing on the roof of a gaily coloured craft, with one lazy eye would notice Roderick out among the buttercups or a pretty girl about her chores. Most probably he would yawn, stretch his hands behind his head, and shut his eyes, quite unaware of the small, neatly painted signs on the river bank: signs vainly advertising Roderick and Osbert's fine fresh honey.

Osbert and Roderick each had a daughter. Both were beautiful girls despite all the hard work and the ragged clothes they had to put up with. True, both were a little on the thin side, but then there was not much food to spare.

Suddenly, one day an incredible change occurred on the banks of the Slyme. At first, boats in ones and twos began to call at Roderick's quay. And before long, lengthy queues of barges and yachts stretched away down river. Eager jostling crowds of traders and travellers were seen on their way, balancing wobbly pots of Roderick's honey. Before long Roderick's daughter Annabel had put on weight and dressed herself in the latest fashions: how beautiful she looked! Roderick built a longer quay and treated himself to more hives and an extra swarm; but best of all, he could now afford to have special labels printed for his pots. —Every label bore the proud words:
  *RODERICK'S REMARKABLE
  HOME-MADE HONEY.*

Of course, the fame of Roderick's honey spread the length of the Slyme — and beyond. No self-respecting traveller would dream of passing Roderick's little white farmhouse without calling in for a couple of jars of this remarkable home-made honey. That would have been quite unthinkable. Naturally, Roderick became very rich indeed.

Osbert remained penniless. Not that he begrudged his old friend his sudden riches: his bad temper owed more to not understanding the cause of Roderick's success. Osbert too sold home-made honey; he too had a neat little sign on the river bank; yet nobody ever stopped to buy *his* honey. Osbert's temper was not helped by his daughter Marigold. She envied Annabel her lovely new clothes and she had seen her eating a *whole* cream cake to herself. Marigold badgered and nattered her father to visit Roderick, in order to discover the secret of riches from the sale of home-made honey.

At last she wore Osbert down and for the sake of peace and quiet he made the short trip across the meadow to Roderick's house. There was a richness about the old place, which he barely recognized. He passed row upon row of freshly painted hives and admired the fine pot gnomes

in front of the gracious new verandah. He felt like a beggar at the door as, with heavy heart, he took off his cap and thumped upon the magnificent brass door knocker.

"Roderick, old friend, let me into the secret of your success," he pleaded.

Roderick thought about this very carefully as he wound his solid gold pocket watch. He gazed at his neighbour's old ragged jacket and, remembering how hard life used to be, at last replied.

"Well it *is* a secret, Bert, but as we've been good neighbours for so long, old chap, I'll give you a clue. The secret of my success lies in the buttercups."

There was a long silence as Osbert's temper rose.

"I've not come here to be insulted!" he cried. "A buttercup is a buttercup, wherever it is! Your buttercups are the same as mine! A buttercup's a buttercup in anybody's language! I'll not be taken for a fool. You'll see, your secret will be out soon enough!"

With that he stormed off, giving the door a mighty slam. Roderick shrugged.

"A pity," he muttered and, for old time's sake, called through the windows, "Study the buttercups, my friend — they can tell you so much!"

The slow summer months passed by and Roderick grew even richer. Almost every boat pulled in for his famous honey. None of the travellers even bothered to glance at Osbert's sign, though it clearly stated that his honey was cheaper than next door's.

One day, leaning on his boundary fence, Osbert called to a traveller who was returning to his boat clutching a pot of honey. "A word in your ear, if you please!"

"It's not for sale," the traveller said, hugging the pot tightly to his chest. "You'll just have to queue like all the rest."

"That's just it," Osbert sighed gloomily. "I've honey in plenty and my honey is just as good — it's cheaper too. So how come everyone stops at Roderick's farm and never at mine?"

"I don't know," the young man shrugged. "Must have been the buttercups, I suppose."

"Buttercups!" Osbert exploded. He was so amazed at this answer that he let the young man go without asking him what exactly he had meant by this remark.

Osbert walked thoughtfully towards his farmhouse, then he had an idea. He gathered a capful of buttercups and carried them indoors.

"Marigold," he called. "Take the petals from these buttercups and we'll mix them in honey."

Marigold thought this was a stupid idea, but since her father looked determined and had been so cross lately, she reluctantly obeyed. Osbert fastened an old mincing machine to the wooden table and began to shred the petals for all he was worth (which wasn't much). When he'd finished, he stirred the yellow mush into a jar of honey. With a triumphant grin he spread the mixture on a slice of bread.

"Here, Marigold, try this," he chuckled.

"Not likely, *you* try it." Marigold shuddered.

Osbert took a huge bite and turned sickly green. He needed to drink seven cups of camomile tea to take away the awful taste.

In the afternoon he had another idea. He wandered into the meadow to pick more buttercups and, as he did so, he saw Roderick give him a cheery wave, calling: "That's it, Bert, study the buttercups — they can tell you so much."

"Grrr!" Osbert glared at Roderick and carried an armful of buttercups over to his hives. He had the idea that the bees could use them to improve their honey. Osbert began to ram and stuff buttercups into the hives. Sadly, the bees did not appreciate his scheme and a fierce swarm chased him indoors. Their angry buzzing kept Osbert there until evening, by which time he had another plan. He smiled to himself as he rubbed those itching bee stings — this had to be the answer.

Next day he rummaged around in an oak chest and fetched out some old clothes. He cut up Marigold's black wig for a false moustache and borrowed her black beret. He raided the pantry for a string of onions and, disguised as a French onion-seller, sneakily joined the queue at Roderick's quay. He had to sell the onions, though Marigold wouldn't be pleased, in order to keep up the disguise. But in the end he bought a jar of Roderick's honey without being recognized and slipped away home with his prize. He quickly shed his disguise and when Marigold came in, he blindfolded her at the wooden table.

"Now," he said solemnly, carefully spreading honey from separate jars on different pieces of bread, "which is mine? And which is Rod's?"

But Marigold couldn't tell the difference and nor could Osbert—without a blindfold.

"Yet Roderick is *very* rich and I am *very* poor," Osbert sighed, "so there *must* be an answer."

That night, his itching stings kept him awake and made his temper worse. Since he could not work out his neighbour's secret, Osbert hatched a dark plot against him.

Next day he cycled thirteen miles to the nearest town, where he spent all his savings in the pet shop. He didn't pause for breath, but cycled straight back home with a small cage resting on his handlebars.

In his kitchen, quite out of breath, he fed two beautiful bee-eaters in their cage. They gobbled the fattest bees Osbert could bring them. He waited until twilight and then, in the soft dusk, slipped unseen with the cage around the back of Roderick's hives. With a wicked chuckle, he released the birds and sneaked off without a backward glance. If he *had* glanced backwards, he would have seen the bee-eaters following him home: they liked him—he gave them fat bees.

Next morning was sunny and Osbert was fed up.

"Oh Marigold," he said, "life can be a misery when you have a bee in your bonnet. Come on, let's take the day off. We'll have a picnic in the rowing boat on the river."

Away he pulled, past rows of moored boats tied to Roderick's quay. As they drew level with Roderick's meadow, to their astonishment, in huge bold yellow letters made up entirely of buttercups and standing out brilliantly against the long meadow grass, were the words ...